The Story of Stories!

Poetry

Nkwazi N. Mhango

Mwanaka Media and Publishing Pvt Ltd,
Chitungwiza, Zimbabwe
*
Creativity, Wisdom, and Beauty

Publisher: *Mmap*
Mwanaka Media and Publishing Pvt Ltd
24 Svosve Road, Zengeza 1
Chitungwiza, Zimbabwe
mwanaka@yahoo.com
mwanaka13@gmail.com
https://www.mmapublishing.org
www.africanbookscollective.com/publishers/mwanaka-media-and-publishing
https://facebook.com/MwanakaMediaAndPublishing/

Distributed in and outside N. America by African Books Collective
orders@africanbookscollective.com
www.africanbookscollective.com

ISBN: 978-1-77933-847-1
EAN: 9781779338471

© Nkwazi N. Mhango 2024

All rights reserved.
No part of this book may be reproduced or transmitted in any form or by any means, mechanical or electronic, including photocopying and recording, or be stored in any information storage or retrieval system, without written permission from the publisher

DISCLAIMER
All views expressed in this publication are those of the author and do not necessarily reflect the views of *Mmap*.

Acknowledgments

I tremendously acknowledge my family
My wife Nesaa
You've always been helpful
You've been by me everyday
Nesaa
You made this work delightful
Never had you felt tired
To every couplet you listened
Sometimes, you had to read and proofread
Thanks for such a big and helpful heart
Hongea Mnaa

To our kids Ng'ani, Nkuzi, and Nkwazi Jr
You've always been our pleasure
You allowed me time to explore
Thanks for understanding
You betcha

Table of Contents

Acknowledgments

Hark My Story Our Story

Is It Salvation or Curse?

Our Story Their Story

Our Story

Their Story

Pauperising Miracles

Let's Rewrite Our History

Self-deniers

Let's Fix Eyes on the Prize

Are We Truly Beggars?

A Holy Jinx

In the Name of Religion

What Is in the Names?

Geographic Baptism

Tell the Story to Every Creature

Goofy and Spoofy Languages

Our Identity

Racism

Bible Vs Land

Mental Slavery

In the Name of God

So Long

    Mmap New African Poets Series

Preface

The Story of Our Stories is the lamentation about why our stories were colonised, demonised, and lastly destroyed. It challenges victims of colonisation to wake up and recoup their bungled and fangled narratives alongside their history based on their factuality, historicity, and naturality. It chides victims to write their histories and tell their stories instead reading and telling the stories their vanquisher miswrote and misconstrued to bolster damnation and domination.

The Story of Stories seeks to decolonise history, geography, land, mind, stories and the entire psyche of victims all over they are.

It catechises, disgraces, and decolonises, some established tawdry colonial dogmas and dregs, which swivel around coloniality and cultural imperialism. Essentially, the book acts as a wakeup call for victims to liberate themselves instead of keeping believing in baloney and hooey at the detriment and even for their jeopardy.

Let the victims, collectively, together, and in unison tell *The Story of Stories*.

Hark My Story Our Story

The story I bring is ours
It is about us
My story your story
My story her story
My story his story
My story our story
I bring you a sad story
It is the story that killed our grand story
It is the story of bigotry
That is its anatomy
It starts with infamy
That revolves around criminality
Aye
The story of destruction of our history
Done for the benefit of their history
It is the story of stories
Listen to the story
The story of stories

If you don't know your story
You will believe even fake stories
If you don't know your history
You will be taught wrong history
If you don't know who you are
Anybody will tell you who you are
Anybody'll create and cast you
Your history and story make you who you are
Your victory makes you victor

Always history is written by a victor
Your history is not just history
Your history is your future
It is your past that created the present
So says the story of stories

The story tells the story of hegemony
Don't deem it blasphemy
We need to delve into our collective memory
Then, let's face our common enemy
True
Let us revisit the story of history
The story of our antiquity
Let us re-examine the historicity of our history
The story of his-story construed as history
His story is his story but not history
It is just like our history
Our history before the destruction
That they heinously called salvation
Our true butchered history and story
The story of stories

Likewise, this is the story of infamy
Let us exhume its litany
It is full of vulgarity
Of those whose story was slew
Those are her and you
Yea, you and I
We are the victims of this criminality
We who are fighting for dignity

Although we are famed for our generosity
This time is perfect
Courageously and collectively, let's face the reality
Let us collectively explore our historicity
As it revolves around colonialism and coloniality
To new generations we must impart and inculcate
All myths we must masticate
Let us our history liberate
How will we do that?
It is through our story of stories
Let's study and tell the story of stories

Peaceable as we have always been
Generous as we have always been
Through them we lost our adoration
We invite everybody
We end up with vainglory
All come and exploit us
This seems to be our sin
Take this allegory
Re-examining our history is mandatory
Again
Should we repeat the slipups again?
With such mishaps what will we gain?
Yet, it is still fine
Our boundaries to redefine
We need to revisit everything again
Yep, we need to refine
All lies pummelled against us
Against our story of stories

Exhume the story of stories

I call upon academics
I invoke activists
Come educate our people
Teach them their story
Reveal their slain history
Show them the way
Come join the fray
Let us exhume our hidden history
Let us tell how it was fell
Let's this story tell
Tell it to every creature
Tell it to even the heavens
Tell it even to the oceans
Fearlessly, tell the story
Our story
Their story
The story of stories

Now, let me tell the real story
The real deal and an in-thing
Nothing will stop our yearning
We need back our civilisation
It is through this history of history
Let's see if it is a curse or salvation
What salvation brought to the victims?
Should we call it cursed salvation?
I don't understand this salvation
Salvation full of agony

Surely, for perpetrators
Call it the story of salvation
In truth, it a story infamy
The story of inanity
This is the very story
The very story of stories

We need to revive the history of Africa
The mother of everything
Didn't Egypt teach them science?
Didn't Ethiopia teach them farming?
Didn't the Masai teach them animal husbandry?
Didn't the concept of one God start in Meroe?
Who built grand Egyptian pyramids?
Don't we know the Nubians did?
What new did our tormentors invent?
So poses the story of stories

Go study the history of embalmment
The first notion you will get is Egypt
Study even irrigation
It all started in Africa
Go even today to rural Africa
Orthopaedics is even performed by young boys
and girls
What does this say?
Africa is the cradle of everything
Despite their lies
They still admit this truth
So reveals the story of stories

Although our violators laugh at us
They openly and systematically hate us
For how long will they fool us?
What is wrong with us?
They thought we made silly decisions
They forgot one obvious reality
They didn't step into our shoes
They would have known the reasons
Why they hoodwinked our descendants
They're not dolts
Neither were they docile
Let us connect the dots
Our ancestors were not imbeciles
They were as smart as a snare
Their goof was their trust
Notes our story of stories

Is It Salvation or Curse?

Let us explore salvation
Who doesn't like salvation?
I mean salvation not cursed salvation
When our tormentors came with their fiction
They hoodwinked us with salvation
We were filled with vain elation
We started dying for heaven
Yet, we ignore our civilisation
We hated our ways of life
What a goof!
Who's ever gone to the heaven?
They called wealth mundane
Yet, they amassed mammon!
They became rich because of their salvation
It was because of our damnation
Shamelessly, they said that is salvation
Did they mean slavation?
Was it cultural lavation?
Did they imply starvation?
Maybe, they meant metaphoric mental
sterilisation!
Aye, cursed is this sort of salvation
The salvation that ended up being our burden
Which lighten their burden
Please, carefully, listen to the story of salvation
It is the story of a great misery
Yea, the story of stories

This is the story of a great dupery
The author of our collective melancholy
We believed our arch enemy
We accepted debauchery
It is time to expose it
Let me say it flatly
No flattery
Salvation or misery?
Yeah, this is my tragic story
It is also your catastrophic story
It is the story of salvation without salvation
It is the story of humiliation
The story of exploitation
The story of corruption
The story of inhumanity
Told by the story of stories

I am telling a story
The story full of history
True history
The history of collective misery
I will tell it again and again
Despite my great pain
Despite my agony
I will tell the story
I will tell it plainly
It is the story of moral corruption
The story of economic deprivation
The story of cultural colonisation
Yep,

It is the story of miseries
The miseries we have suffered for generations
Now, it is time
To tell this story to the new generation
So that they can take actions
Indeed, they need to take decisive actions
So says the story of stories

Hark this very story
My story
Your story
Our collective story
A story full of melancholy
Your preposterous story
Our glum and doomed story
The story of stories
Ay
Our story of their stories
The story of their barbarities
The story of deceits
The story of cultural absurdities
The story of asymmetricities
This is the story of stories

I bring the erased story of ours
The story of yours
The story of his and hers
Let us revisit our story
Let us remind each other
Yo

Let us talk about our story
We need to reclaim our story
This is our sacred allegory
We need to revive our collective memory
Let's tell our lost story
Let us tell this holy story
Let's tell it with sheer bravery
Tell the story of stories

Let us seek it like gold
Let us keep it like diamond
Let us remove all mold
Let us tell it boldly
Our story is grand
Our story is a brand
Our story is our rock
We who were turned into a laughingstock
Let us take stock
This is for every folk
We have a myth to debunk
We must do so chunk by chunk
Seriously, this isn't a joke
Let's boldly tell the story of stories

Before telling our story
Let me tell their story
The story that swallowed our story
The story of chicanery
The one that demonised our story
The story of savagery

Savagery called civilisation
The one shaped and maintained by trickery
It is very slippery
We must exhume it carefully
Despite its cruelty
We still need to tell it
Victims must know it
Through the truth of the story of stories

This is not the wars of stories
Neither is it the competition of stories
It is the peep into realities
The realities of two major stories
Their story and our story
Those who miswrote our story
Those who demonised our story
They also need to read this story
It is their story
Yea
Our collective story of stories
The story of stories

Our Story Their Story

I humbly and proudly beg to tell a story
Through storytelling I tell the story
This is nothing but a promissory of delivery
A noble and true story
The story of victims and perpetrators
It is the story of the humanity
It calls for the entire humanity
It seeks to right all wrongs
The wrongs ones committed against others
The story that bothers
The story that distresses
The story of victims and criminals
This is nothing but our story of stories

This is but the story of trepidation
It is told without any sensation
It is our realisation
That we need to do something
The story that involves crucifixion
Yea, I say crucifixion
It a promissory of false benediction
In reality it is the crucifixion of Africans
It is the crucifixion of all victims
The story of how we're turned into ruffians
Aye, turned into ruffians by ruffians
They duped us with religions
We lost our civilisations

Then, they called our loss salvation
As told by the story of stories

How can there be salvation amidst vulnerability?
Can there be salvation amidst quandaries and
miseries?
How can salvation be brought through depravity?
Didn't the salvation create our inferiority?
Didn't it ward them superiority?
Where is cultural equality?
Where is political equity?
Where is impartiality?
Where is reciprocity?
How can salvation come by the way of
criminality?
What do you call that?
Did cultural imperialism bring any salvation?
Whose salvation?
Who needs such salvation?
Let us ask this great question
Whose salvation?
Ask the story of stories

They came salivating for our prosperity
They employed all sorts of trickery
These criminals devoid of any dignity
These humans without any quality of humanity
They perfunctorily said they brought morality
Did they have any morality?
Nay

What they had and knew was criminality
With an unexplainable deceit
With unimaginable cruelty
They occupied our society
They destroyed our development
As enumerated in the story of stories

Aren't our animals better than us?
Look at birds
They have their nests
Look at snakes and lizards
They have their mounds
What do we have as humans?
They came talking about animal protection
They campaign for endangered species
What of endangered Africans?
Environmental protection
Where is human protection?
Where is Africa's compensation?
Ay
Africa deserves compensation against injustices
Who committed all such injustices?
We need justice
So admonishes the story of stories

Here we are disdained
Amidst their salvation we are cursed
We collectively are discriminated against
What a disgust!
All started after we were pauperised

It was after we were duped
Yea
After we were robbed
Here we are pointlessly aided
As if we did not have any resources
It happened after our kin conspired
To the free market we were vended
We lost everything we treasured
Here we are favoured
We depend on handouts
Despite sitting on humungous resources
Yep
Resources of great value
Whom do they benefit?
A few of our homemade traitors?
Exhumed by the story of stories

Are we real poor to be feed by those we feed?
What's the meaning of all resources with which we're endowed?
We pride ourselves of having one of the biggest continents
We pride ourselves of having vast sources of resources
Yet, we live in unimaginable miseries!
Are we useless so as to be aided by those we aid?
Who is fooling whom including oneself?
Don't our torturers know this plain truth?
Don't they export to us what the make out of our products?

What do we get out of their products?
Do they have any?
Why don't they face the reality then?
For how long with this disdain?
What do we gain?
Ask the story of stories

They extend aid to us
They call it economic salvation
How much do they rob from us?
They call such criminality commerce
Is it not a crime against Africans?
Is it not the crime against humanity?
What should we call it?
Ironically and sadly
They call it free market
Aye
Freebooting
Free syphoning
Free profiteering
Still, they call everything salvation!
Contrary to the story of stories

Our economies feed theirs
Theirs feed on ours
Instead of reciprocating
They also rob us
They use our own brothers and sisters
Those in the upper echelons of power
Before their masters they cower

Despite having power
They become powerless
Despite having brains
They became brainless
Our rulers serve their leaders
Our people ape everything that's theirs
Yet, they despise everything that's ours
They call this inequity international relations
Why do we make do with this?
Don't we see it?
Don't they know it?
Let us address this fallacy
Through telling the story of stories

They call their countries developed
Ours are un or underdeveloped
They define development
We receive their bungled definitions
We do not question
We do not ever protest
Even when we are mistreated
Even when we are offended
We pretend
Everything is spiffy
It is very nifty
Though it is different in the story of stories

This is the story I proudly tell
I will tell it with nerves of steel
This is the story of how we fell

Despite all
My aim is to heal
Also, I need to the truth to reveal
For me, this is but a big deal
Yea, a real deal
I have a story to tell
This is the story for all
The story of stories

We need to examine it afresh
To see what we can accomplish
We are tired of the hell
The hell we had to embellish
Let us say that we no longer want to perish
We need our story to cherish
Again
How under hush?
Can they hush the story of stories?

We need to make noises
Sometimes, it need some ruckus
To understand the significance of peace
Our story is the story of peace
Even though we suffered violence
We never wished vengeance
We abhor violence
We are loving persons
We love even our enemies
This is our story
Ay, the story of stories

Their story is the story of violence
Theirs is the story of delinquency
Theirs is a bloodstained story
Ours is the bloodletting story
Yet, both are stories
We need to tell these stories
We need to listen to these stories
They are our stories
However different they are
This is who we are
As told by the story of stories

Through telling our story and their story
We aim to demolish the house of cards
We intend to defeat fibs
Our stories are not fads
Let's defend it with all available intellectual jabs
It is through excavating our story
Our true story
Let us tell it without any gabs
Love and truth are the gibs
Those that keep it together
Let us stand together
And tell the story of stories

Come join me to listen to the story
Since it is our story
Let us come together
Let us talk to each other
We need to collectively realise

That we still need each other
Even if we offended each other
Our stories will always link us together
However uglier they are
They still are our stories
All wrapped in the story of stories

Our Story

I am telling the story of a big damage
A generational great demise
Loss of everything
Loss in any meaning
Loss of our being
Loss of our glory
I still feel very sorry
When I see how this dupery
Has been ongoing
As if we're tabula rasa
Contrary to the story of stories

This is our story
I put it adjacent to their story
It is the story of victory
The story of resilience
It is the story of forgiveness
That begs for openness
It is the story of genuineness
That begs for positive reciprocity
It is the story of integrity
Let us support it
This is for us monumental
It is the story of our stories

Many years ago
There once came a people
They were highway men who came from far away

To be exact
They came from Europe
They seemed to be humble
Although, they were horrible
They committed horrible things
What they did is indescribable
Although we let bygone go
As admonishes the story of stories

Their criminality is unimaginable
They came and duped our people
They robbed them of everything profitable
They destroyed their ways of life
They brought strife
They brought grief
It is deplorable
Our people still glorify this waffle
What an obvious bluff!
As exhumed by the story of stories

There came a white man with 'salvation'
Aye, the curse of salvation
He brought paganism
He brought colonialism
Yet, he called it civilisation
We lost our civilisation
As we took on his civilisation
We since suffered from indignation
Since then, we've lived under domination

Everything we held dear has suffered from condemnation
Hark the story of stories

After the 'white' pinky man
There came a submission man
You know what I mean
Yep, no-no
He who says everything is hers or his
Even what is not hers or his
Despite all her or his braggadocios
He was also colonised
He too had us culturally colonised
We carry his names
We postulate towards his place
Yet, he misses in the story of stories!

He and the white one sold us
They gave their names to us
They culturally demonised us
Though we think they're enemies
They are in the same base
They secretly see us as their slaves
Ay, we are if we don't rebel
If we don't relinquish their labels
Aye, their ideological medals
The ones that have kept us asunder
As shamed by the story of stories

How can cursed people save innocuous people?
Whoever on this honestly and seriously ponders
Must give us nothing but correct answers
How can criminals save righteous people?
How can sinners save innocent people?
How can dirty people sanitise clean people?
How can darkness save the light?
How can a thief save a property title-holder?
How can wickedness save virtuousness?
How can criminality save guiltlessness?
So queries the story of stories

How do you call that?
Is it not the curse of salvation?
Salvation in what?
While we lost our civilisation
We suffered from cruel and cultural annihilation
Yet, we sung salvation
Is this salvation or cultural starvation?
Isn't this self-destruction hidden
In the name of salvation
This is how curse became salvation
as exhumed by the story of stories

Their Story

This is the story of white men
Evil and callous men
Those who duped us
Those who robbed us
Those who tortured
Of all
They told lies about us
I must make it crystal flawless
Not all white people are evil and malicious
Those who colonised were really callous
They came humbly
We mistook them of angles
What devils!
All happenings were like a chain of events
Those that took place among us
Yea
We need to know every bit
Since it is about us
We didn't know they were bullies
We didn't know they were criminals
Heartless criminals
Yeah, they bullied us
They enslaves us
They colonised us
They're still colonising us
As per the story of stories

Since then we have suffered valiantly

Economic slavery
Political slavery
Cultural slavery
And of all
Everything immaturity
They brought and exacerbated poverty
They turned a self-dependent people into dependent
Then, they called that development
They gave us a moniker of a developing society
As disputed by the story of stories

They overthrew and destroyed our prosperous kingdoms
They even cloned fake ones they used against powerful domains
They hanged our Kings and Queens
They installed their damn administrations
Call it colonisation
They forced us to embark on liberation
Then, they made an assertion
That they gave us our autonomy
They introduced their dirty government
They called them democracies
Were they democracies?
We're not as per the story of stories

Ironically, after killing our Kings and Queens
They started teaching us love
After enslaving us and making big profits

They started preaching love and equality
After pauperising us
They started preaching economic competition
After revealing our secrets to them
They started proclaiming inventions
After feeding them
They started to claim they saved us from
starvation
After copying and lifting our knowledges
They started calling us ignorant
After teaching them civilisation
They called us savages
So notes the story of stories

They assigned themselves development
Everything good became theirs
Their culture became dominant
Ours became dormant
Their dirty cultures they exported to us
Their criminality they exported to us
Whatever they did became a sort of advancement
Their crimes became source of their prosperity
They called theirs a developed society
Ours became the third world
Theirs the first world
Sadly, we internalised everything
As admonishes the story of stories

They made us act crazy

They shamelessly introduced their crazy
democracy
Politics crated chaos
Brutally, religions made our people lazy
Now, they are accusing us of being lazy
Before them we are but ditzy
Whatever we do is but zilch
We are but crazy and klutzy
They deceitfully appointed themselves our oracles
They taught our people to depend on miracles
People have stopped working harder
They have banked in gimmicks and miracles
They want to go to heaven
Yet, they are not ready to die
Says the story of stories

Religions have robbed our people
Yet, they call it a miracle
Indeed, it is a miracle
They say their God is wealthy
He makes people rich
Then, they tax the poor!
Why doesn't their God make them rich?
They ask for offerings
Why doesn't they cater for their needs?
Ask the story of stories

Our people are swindled
They are pauperised
They offer abundantly

Wrongly thinking they offer to God
God doesn't need your moneys
God needs nothing
God must provide everything
Even for those purporting to be his envoys
Why should we feed them?
Did we employ them?
Ask the story of stories

Politics also made us indolent
A few corrupt creatures use it to rob others
Like arty preachers
They feed them words
They become abruptly opulent
It brought collective obliteration and insolvency
Nations are now becoming panhandlers
Despite sitting on vast reserves
They've become beggars from other nations
Colonisers made us insignificant
They created unimaginable absurdity
Every five years
We fight each other
We call it votes
We choose the eaters
Those who pretend to represent us
Instead, they represent their tummies
They represent their families
Their parties
Their masters
All have betrayed us

They have vended us
As Alan Paton put it
Cry the beloved country
I say that cry every African country
Ja, this is the story of stories

Pauperising Miracles

When the 'people' of God came
They brought cataclysm
They invented miracles
The power that makes fortunes without thinking
One can become rich without toiling
Again
If you ask how many
It is only those who swindle others preaching fake miracles
If there are miracles
They are nothing but duping those seeking miracles
Another miracle is with the authorities
Don't they make do with such cons and criminals?
Why?
They all perform miracles of reaping where they didn't sow
This is what the story of stories teach us
Read the story of stories

Because of the hypnotising power of miracles
People no longer work hard
Instead, they pray hard
They pray for bread
Then
They wait for the miracles

Do you know the miracles?
They are openly robbed
Miraculously, they don't complain
Is it not a miracle?
So ask the story stories

Conmen and women prey on them so hard
It is as if they have lost their minds
They have refused to work with their hands
Instead, they pray for manna from heaven
And wait for godsend
They pray for miracles
They are always in mental manacles
Fake miracles have replaced hard work
Faiths have turned many victims into a laughingstock
Foreign faiths are illusory
They are purely discriminatory
Blessed are their harbingers
And cursed are their religious holders
So says the story of stories

Conmen and women cheat victims that they can perform miracles
They allege that they can cure sick people
Ironically, when they become ill
They run to the hospital
They stage shows to prove their fake miracles
Why do they do that?
How'll they rob unsuspected targets?

They boast that they can expel demons
How can demons expel demons?
Where do demons live?
What qualities do they have?
So queries the story of stories

Religious cons taught our people to speak in the gobbledegook tongues
Despite speaking in tongues
hey are eaten like togues
Their beliefs are openly vague
Since they received these harangues
Did they ask their meanings?
Do they understand their coded messages?
To make matters worse
Some of us started to regurgitate such enigmas
Nay!
Many criminals are now politicians
They have even hijacked academicians
All have joined hands
In eating the earthlings
As exhumed by the story of stories

Let's Rewrite Our History

We need to rewrite the history of history
We must do so to reclaim our history
Just like we want to do to our story
We need to teach our true history
We need to decolonise our history
So, too our story
We need both decolonised history and story
We must shun his-story that he called history
Doing so is a big and thunderous victory
It is victory against purgatory
We need to form a collective decolonised memory
By and with it we can decolonise ourselves
collectively
This is our collective sacred duty
To tell the story of stories

As Ngugi wa Thiong'o was proposed
He said that we need to decolonise our minds
Chinua said things fell apart
Mandela taught us long walk to freedom
Odinga gave us not yet uhuru
Additionally, I must say it
We need to decolonise our land
We need to decolonise our streets
We need to decolonise our countries
I know how pregnant they are with foreign
effigies

It is full of colonial monuments
It is time we decolonise everything
Let us decolonise ourselves
Through understanding our story of stories

With golden ink to write our story
Let us think together about how to reclaim our story
Alongside our story is our history
Let this be the story of history
We too need to rewrite our history
We need to present it afresh
Let revival be our approach
The mission we'll accomplish
Those who miswrote and misrepresented must be shamed
Let us exhume the validity
Let's shame the fibbers
So says the story of stories

Self-deniers

I see self-denial ubiquitously
What is it?
Do I have to define it?
Seriously?
Self-denial is victims' botch
All but hogwash
Devoured sheepishly
Trusted religiously
While it is nothing but vile
What a valued bagatelle!
As per our story of stories

How many discriminate themselves?
Don't they lighten their skin colour?
What is wrong with their natural colour?
How much money do they burn on this damage?
Don't our governments allow dangerous
chemicals for skin lightening?
What should we call this malady?
Isn't it self-hatred and self-discrimination?
Again, who defines beauty globally?
What is the root cause of this anomaly?
Never seek far
Everything white was made superior
Everything black was made inferior
This is the source of self-discrimination
So says the story of stories

We need to remove this colour mask
This is our sacred task
It is the sacred duty for us, for ourselves
How do we trust those who produce such contaminants?
Don't we import such waste?
Ironically, we spend hard earned forex
Currently, we are losing many souls
Those who go for beauty surgery
They can increase anything in their bodies
Yet, we call this freedom of choice
Why do we ignore the risks?
So marvels the stories of stories

Self-denialism is a failure
It is binary by nature
I see the perpetrator
So, too, I see the survivor
They are all together
Yet, I see no saviour
They spuriously hug each other
For the peril of the other
And the rejuvenation of the other
Of the two, the 'lamb' is the loser
Exhumes our story of stories

What a limbo!
Everyone is but a himbo
Especially, when one believes in mumbo-jumbo
Any tormentor think a victim is a bimbo

What a scriligo!
What boondoggle!
We ignored even our sages
What did we get out of this garbage google?
To which everybody is a doogle
Is there anything for us about which to giggle?
Nothing, as per our story of stories

Ironically, denialism involve many people
Some are even highly knowledgeable
Yet, they swallow such boondoggle
It is like a faithful and loving couple
Or like priest and a head capped bimbo
Don't you see them in their swindle?
Who questions this open hush-hush?
Ghosh!
This hogwash
Just trash
Says the story of stories

See how priests cheat us
Some elope with our wives
Many have defiled our boys and girls
How many court cases they now face?
Go ask the Vatican
Despite its mess
They called it the Holy See
Holy or gory see?
Is it not grappling with its adulterous priests?
They even deceive themselves

They talk about celibacy
They curse adultery
Yet, they commit it even more those they reprove
Is there any celibacy really?
Why do they live close to nuns?
What does that mean?
How many babies they precipitously destroy?
How many marriages do they surreptitiously ruin?
Who doesn't know such plain truth?
Yet, they say they can forgive sins!
Never as testifies the story of stories

How can sinners forgive peccadillos?
How can winos be teachers of leaders?
I openly say it
Hear it
Listen to it
No forgiveness can come from sinners
No salvation can come from sinners
They are sinners per se
This doesn't need any excuse
Is this what they call miracles?
Of which is to fit others with manacles
Do you remember?
Original sin
Who started this sin?
Did we ask this question?
When we're branded us sinners?
Evidences the story of stories

Let us ask a million question now
Let's do it fearlessly
Let's pursue it persistently
Who's the wherewithal to forgive sins?
Between these criminals and the victims
This is the biggest question we need to pose
We must be given correct and reasonable response
Let's reclaim our voices
Let's rise our voices
The time is now
Listen to the story of stories

Isn't adultery not their original sin?
The sin that they superimposed on their victims
Yeah, unsuspecting victims
That is a sacrilegious sin
It is an outrageous bane
They said Adam and Eve committed it
They said that Eve was made out of Adam's rib
Whom do they turn into a goob?
That is one of their fibs
How come that all humans come from women's wombs?

Yet, they kept on committing it
They cheat people that they can forgive the sin they commit
Who knew priests who are proved pedophiles?
Who knew nuns could be doxies?

What a hoax!
What a jinx!
It is as per the story of stories

Where exactly were Adam and Eve originated?
Their historians tell us Africa is the cradle of humanity
Europe is the cradle of coloniality
Due to their confusion and ignorance
They say the Middle East is the cradle of civilisation
How if everything started in Africa?
This is the question we need to ask gallantly
So encourages the story of stories

Who wants salvation through curse?
Curse will always be curse
The two shall never mix
Although they have been in the mix
I say nix
Is this salvation or humiliation?
What a jinx!
I say no to this jinx
Things need a fix
Then, what next?
Ask the story of stories

Let us right the wrong
The gauntlet has been thrown
We must turn over all stones
Let us shame their fake thrones

We must examine every speck
Even those we wrongly think
Those we think were written in stones
They are nothing but fables
Hooeys
Baloney
Sheer malarkey
Let us do things proudly
We must overstep the normalised bounds
Let's clean all that had us plagued
Admonishes the story of stories

Let's Fix Eyes on the Prize

Let us fix our eyes on the prize
We must pluckily excavate all duplicities
Let's expose their trickeries
Let us show and tell them we're tired
We need to make our case
That we no longer need
Their toxic guidance
Let them know we've matured
We need to stir our fate
Admonishes the story of stories

Why has salvation created dependence?
When will we use our own intelligence?
Religion has fathered decadence
Adultery is now another curse
Priests are facing the music
After violating their droves
Off are the gloves
On us it behooves
We no longer are their slaves
Let's be aggressive and suasive
Let's expose whatever dirty things they do
All of their dodo
Don't they suffer from sexual go-go?
We can't behave like dingoes
Says the story of stories
I see couples in them
don't they share the shame?

Don't they impregnate them?
Where do they dumb those zygotes?
doesn't mean they don't become pregnant?
Do they use preventive pellets?
Don't they know this is evil?
This world!
It is full of wiles!
It is total vilely
Says the story of stories

They are together in denial business
What a fallacy!
Denialism is like a curse
It noshes both accomplices
Alas!
Do they stop their crimes!
Don't the victims make do
with their crimes?
They don't and will nary do
How'd they while they're captivated?
So queries the story of stories

The two live in denialism
One denies duplicity
One denies does not suffer from duplicity
They are all culpable of denialism
Amidst this cultural colonialism
This is nothing but hooliganism
We need to stop it
We need to fight it

So as to reclaim and get our rights
When will we pull them before our courts?
Asks the story of stories

It all goes to euhemerism
From where all isms came
With all bumbling things
Colonialism
Capitalism
Racism
Exploitation
Division
Partition
And neocolonialism
Reminds the story of stories

I am talking of all isms of opportunism
All roots of delinquency
Wickedness
Racism
Neocolonialism
Ism after ism
Tall tale after tall tale
That created our nightmare
Aye, I mean our calamitous future
The future without future
Admonishes the story of stories

They brought us conflict
Before,

We didn't know crusade
We were peaceful
We were trustful
They came with their dishonesty
Jihad
Crusade
Inquisition
Division
Persecution
Those are evils they brought
Says the story of stories

They decorated with fabrications
Remember baptism?
Remember conversion?
Remember fake peace
Didn't they cause violence?
They pretended to preach peace
How could there be peace?
Among divisions
How could there be peace?
In cultural mortification
So queries the story of stories

They created a great sacrilege
We did not know anything
We knew nothing about anomic zoophilia
They created cultural phobia
Our cultures became a pariah
Theirs they iconized

Our pure cultures became dirty
Their dirty cultures became pure
Whose cultures were pure and impure
Consider main cultural traits of every culture
We knew nothing about Gomorrah
We didn't their retributive Torah
We had our beliefs
Our ways of life
They demonised everything
So says the story of stories

Cultural contamination became an issue
They robbed our cultures
They found us with our practices
They took them and called them theirs
Weren't we practising circumcision?
Didn't we know the self-styled writs?
They called them the Ten Commandments
Even our animals did
Consider the behaviour of your dog or cat
When any of them steals something
It will run away on seeing the owner
Isn't this their eighth commandment?
Look at how bulls fight over females
Isn't this their seventh commandment?
What is new here?
Ask the story of stories

Only our land and food survived
Our bodies too survived after being enslaved

Under baptism they were enslaved
Under politics they were colonised
Under business they were caged
They gave us fake independence
Independence in dependence
Begging and borrowing became our means
Yeah
Testifies the story of stories

Are We Truly Beggars?

Despite having vast resources
Our injudicious rulers are but beggars
They even beg for what they plently have
In begging they are brave
Don't we import even toys?
Aren't our old rulers behaving like boys/girls?
What is left of them?
Do they feel any shame?
Don't they defend and swallow bunkum?
As if they are not a society of humans
Quips the story of stories

Shameless they talked about the bestiality
That they committed where they originated
Have we ever complained or condemned?
We could not believe humans could do that
Yet, they admittedly said they committed that
What can such a people teach others?
Despite their flaws
We allowed them to teach us
What did they teach us?
Sheepishness?
Queries the story of stories

The answer is artless
They taught us self-destruction
Is there anything they learn from us?

Aye
They learned we are but heedless
That is why for years
They have kept on feeding us
The same bosh
Aye
They've taught us to shush!
Contends the story of stories

They turned us into zombies
Yea, the one they can coerce
We started fearing and hating ourselves
We continuously keep on hating each other
Aren't our own enemies in this idiocy?
We sabotage each other
Do we bother?
We avoid each other
Do we care?
Why should we care?
Quips the story of stories

We're taught sheepishness
We called that godliness
Despite its uselessness
We still venerated such morass
Isn't this evilness?
They called such criminality salvation
Yea
Salvation by curse
They abused us

They abused our customs
We said amen
Amen *ad infinitum*
Quips the story of stories

Salvation ever since became a motif
Though ugly, for us it is beautiful
Condemnation is called salvation
Curse as well is called salvation
Using the weapon of belief
Our people accepted every provocation
Ironically it goes with a boff
Just the same for a pauper and a toff
Belief has become an inebriation
Everybody can quaff
Says the story of stories

They brought their breads
They condemned our foods
Yet, they devoured them
Some exported them
We didn't suspect them
Didn't they know?
Many Africans do not depend on bread
Some refused to eat the meat they did not slaughter
Did they produce the slaughtered animals?
They taught us how to greet each other
Didn't we have our greetings?
We believed in every trash

As before them we became hogwash
They got whatever they'd to wish
We wrongly put all eggs in the same bucket
What a mistake!
We just did nothing but watch!
Even when all signs indicated we'd perish
We ignore all signs
It is now we're coming to the realisation
We need to study the story of stories

Our tormentors kept on adding things
They brought dress codes
They deemed us all naked
Our females became the biggest victims
They're prohibited even from rising their voice
They're forbidden to appear in public
They've been objectified
We've become acentric
Soon, we'll become lunatics
If you ask why
They say that that is god's writ
Do you get it?
Where was he before they came?
So queries the story of stories

A Holy Jinx

Everything we had was declared sinful
Theirs became heavenly
Despite such obscenity
Despite all carnality
We swallowed unquestionably
The baptised us
They baptised even our places
They were given colonial names
We didn't even oppose!
What a cuss!
We need to decolonise them
We need territorial decolonisation
Material decolonisation
Moral decolonisation
Decolonisation
Decolonisation
And decolonisation
Ask the story of stories

They turned us into lunatics
Before them we are but robots
They free embarked on despoilment
Our resources were decimated
Our cultures were molested
It is time to revolt
We're taught to hate the world
They shamelessly said

Ours should be the paradise
We're taught to become willing paupers

They instilled fear in us
We were taught about the god of vengeance
They introduced their god of fire
God full of threats and anger
We're used to our God of love
Slowly, we became *wapumbavu*
A Swahili word for fools
In German *dummkopfs*
Now, listen to the buff
What did we achieve?
We lost everything
They gained everything
Here I am now complaining

Some covertly or overtly deny their evil deeds
Others blatantly deny their true identity
Others deny even their history
It is as if they're created yesterday
What a dismay!
What an agony!
Who'll save us?
Jesus failed to save us
Religion has failed to save us

When will Jesus save us?
Again, did he come for us?
Why didn't we understand his words?

Didn't he say he came for only Jews
Are we Jews?
Didn't he call us gentiles?

Jesus was miracle maker
Ay
What miracles!
Wasn't he the victim of their miracles?
One of these miracles still holds
Jesus was born a Judean
A Judean who was betrayed by Judas
Yet, for their hidden intentionality
They turned him into a Caucasian
I still even wonder
Why hasn't the world deciphered this fabrication
They took the photos of their actors
Then, they called them Jesus!
How many Jesuses are out there?
Which among them is the real Jesus?
Jesus was born in Palestine
All of the sudden they made him a Judean
Isn't this itself a betrayal?
Wasn't he a Palestinian?
All such questions need correct answers
Who gave them the powers of abrogation?
Is that what they mean by identity transfiguration?
What a fiction!
Ask the story of stories

Wasn't Jesus a victim of identity alteration?

Is that the reason why they maliciously altered our identity?
Who questions Jesus' true identity?
Is such criminality godly?
How many believe in such fabrications?
Fabrications done in the name of God
Shamelessly, they assert it is holy
Holy fib
Holy fix
Holy bugaboo
Holy no-no
The jinx of salvation
This needs a fix
The truth must come out
So says the story of stories

In the Name of Religion

With a heavy breve
We dug our own cultural grave
Faith came by the ways of lies
Lies in the name of God
The logic it defies
This kind of God
Why did they lie to us?
Who bewitched us?
Did they bewitch us?
What is wrong with us?
Faith softened us
Heavens blinded us
Lies duped us
It made it easy for them to colonise us
Yes, missionaries spied on us
Explorers hoodwinked us
The colonisers followed
They easily colonised our land
They grabbed our land
Then, they exploited our blood
So notes the story of stories

They robbed us of freedom
They robbed us of our self-esteem
We had to fight for everything afresh
Many of our heroes and heroines did perish
They endured all sorts of cruelty

Who can forget such bunkum?
The wounds are still fresh
We suffered a lot
We lost a lot
Ironically, God kept quiet
As his people did nothing but us to exploit
Thereafter, they said we are brethren
Brethren in religion!
Why now not then?
Are we brethren?
Brethren in disdain
Then, they said everything was fine!
Brethren cannot enslave brethren
Neither can they colonise their brethren
Where was God then?
Was he in the heaven?
Ask the story of stories

Do our cries reach to the heaven?
If they do
Does their God bother to listen?
Does he hear them
If God does do
Why did he ignore 'his' children?
Are we truly God's children?
Just like those who brought their salvation
Those morons
These loonies
These deadly gooneys
So, probes the story of stories

What Is in the Names?

What is the names?
Let us ponder on names
What I know about names
Just like you do
All names
African names
Foreign names
Are names just names?
No
They have their meanings
Some deny their names
After assuming foreign names
Others avoid their languages
They take others' languages
They embrace others' cultures
Aren't they their own archfoes?
What do you call this?
Do they need a pep talk?
Maybe, they deserve a thwack
So instructs the story stories

When colonisers came
They brought their ludicrous names with them
They butchered our good names
They gave us derisory foreign names
What is in the names?
We need to decolonise our names

We need to toss their names
Let them come and take them
We no longer need them
Their reprehensible names
So quips the story of stories

Its imposing names on us wasn't racism?
Why only foreign names?
Why only foreign narratives?
Why foreign holy places?
I need to know
They brought idols
They taught us to worship them
Then they turn the table on us
They said we worshipped idols
They exempted those they brought to us!
So unearths the story of stories

Wasn't the imposition of names on us identity theft?
What do you call that?
Why only foreign names?
We sheepishly accepted their ridiculous names
After we hated and were robbed of our beautiful names
Meaningful names
Heroic names
Like machines we took upon their dirty names
Aren't we like androids?
Do they question their codes?
Better are the machines

Since they don't have minds
What of the mankind?
Or call it 'womankind
We blindly forgot and ignored our good names
Here now we are crying for names
Let us reclaim our beautiful and meaningful names
So admonishes the story of stories

We sheepishly accepted their names
We proudly carried their ludicrous names
Unquestionably, we accepted Arabic names
European names
All names
Blindly, we sacrificed our names
We started to hate them
As we praised colonial names
Despite all shame
We still carry ridiculous foreign names!
NoViolet Bulawayo says that we need new names
Who else says that?
The story of stories
When colonisers and hyenas came
They called us names
Dirty and foreign ones
We've ever since carried their names
As we abused and denied ours
What a shame!
They do us harm
Yet, we did not retaliate
Should we do that?

This is the time to do that
Like pets
We're given new names
It is as if we didn't have names
What a shame!
What a shame we turned into fame
Sadly, we refused to return back their names
Is it late to reclaim our glorious names?
Let us shun colonial and foreign names
We have our beautiful and meaningful names
What is in the names?

They brought baptism
They said they were purifying us
Were we impure?
Who purified them?
They did that even to babies
Can babies be impure?
Why do they deem them angels?
Yet, they baptise them
Why didn't they baptise our animals?
Ironically, they baptised our land
Many places carry their evil names
Dirty names
What went wrong with us?
Quips the story of stories

They called us Livingstone
They called us Columbus
That criminal that new nothing

The one that lost in Americas in his way to India
They named us David
The criminal who spied on Africa
They called us Stanley
The baseborn who miswrote the history of Africa
Weren't all these criminals?
Weren't the same the harbingers
Those who paved the way for colonialism
They paved the way for cultural domination
They sowed the seeds of our destruction
Yet, shamelessly, they called that salvation
They hyped their original sin as civilisation!
Let us exhume the story of stories

Geographic Baptism

Their deceptive and evil baptism did not end up
with our bodies
They poured waters on our heads
Then
They baptised our lands
The excreted on our lands
Call it geographic toxification
Maybe
It was geographic baptism
Burundi, Rwanda, and Tanganyika were called
German East Africa!
Kenya, Uganda, and Zanzibar were called British
East Africa!
Where was Britain African colony?
Was there any German African colony?
Burkina Faso was baptised Upper Volta an Italian
dirty name
Thomas Sankara came and detoxified his land
He named it Burkina Faso the land of
incorruptible people
Ghana was called Cold Coast
After they robbed it its gold
At independence it reclaimed its glorious name
Mosi-oa-Tunya and Nyanza was renamed Victoria
That criminal Queen of Britannia
Zambia and Zimbabwe were baptised Rhodesia
After the criminal Cecil Rhodes who grabbed it

Bravo
Zimbabwe reclaimed its glorious name
Dzimba dza mabwe
The houses of stones
Zambia did the same
Praise the story of stories

How many places still remain out there?
Whom should we blame?
What stops u from defaming our lands?
For what are we clinging to such gods?
Those baptised with colonial and dirty names
Methinks, they are in millions
What are we waiting for?
Why don't we detoxify them?
Whom are we afraid?
Let us do it today
Let's detoxify our bodies
Let's shed our dirty names
Let us be who we are
Let us refuse to be whom they wanted us to be
We are not animals
We are not mountains
We are not rivers
We are not gauges
Say the story of stories

They taught us cannibalism
Through salvation
We emblematically eat the flesh of Jesus

What kind of symbolisms?
We drink his blood
We praise the rood
Others feel good
That they are the children of God
Which God?
Can God be crude and rude?
Why did he send us creeps?
Those who yclept us sheep
Which God that does not care about our torments?
Queries the story of stories

Do we need to become cannibals while we are rich in animals?
What will our cows, goats and other do?
Do we need somebody's blood to be pure?
Since when the blood became pure?
By the way, are we impure?
What purity can blood bring?
Why don't we drink the blood of our ancestors?
Can their blood purity colonisers?
If we drink blood
What will lions and leopards do?
Even these faunas do not eat the fleshes of their kin
How do we tackle such abnormality?
Ask the story of stories

Let me go back to names

Ay
It is about chicanery baptism
Pets do better than we do
Do you know what they do?
Cool
They don't accept human names
Though foolishly human think they do
You call them
They just briskly look at you
Sometimes, they trick you
They pretend they accepted the names
They fool you to get what they want
Pets are brainy
So says the story of stories

Names have their historicity
They are the future hints
For future cohorts
They are the books of history
The books of meanings
The nodes for the future and the past
Names are not ornaments
Sometimes, names can be predictors
They tell what is covert
They are like chronometers
So, don't ignore the significance of names
Names shape our identity
They tell our story
Even before we tell it
If names were insignificant

Our tormentors wouldn't have bothered with
calling us theirs
They did so because of their huge their
significance
Names are not just names
Never take your African names like banes
They have their meanings
So says the story of stories

Everything that our tormentors killed
It tells you it was important
If it were insignificant
They would not have bothered about it
All those things you trivialise
You must realise
They are so significant
Reclaim them at any cost
One of the wealth we lost
It is nothing but our beautiful names
Our meaningful names
Let us reclaim our names
So admonishes the story of stories

Our names are like books
They tell our stories
They tell when we were born
Where we were born
Shun all names of crooks
Foreign names make us look like chooks
Let us stop being treated like mooks

Before them we are like kooks
We are nothing but boobooks
Nope
Let's criminalise superimposed names
So says the story of stories
I better be Nkwazi but not Livingstone
I better be Nkuzi but not Samson
How if I am not Hebrew?
Am I a stone to carry such a name?
I better be Nkosi but not Jason
I better be proud of Nesaa
This is a noble name
I better be Ng'ani but not Alison
How can I be Jason without any meaningful salvation?
Some of our people were named Peter
Were they rocks?
Why call me David as if I am Jew?
Why call me Mahamat as if I am Arab?
Do those whose names we carry use our names?
Where is cultural parity?
Where is cultural reciprocity?
Go ask the story of stories

Tell the Story to Every Creature

Please go tell your story
Tell it gallantly
Even if is miswritten
Even if it is misrepresented
Just go tell it
Expose their deception
That they hid in their books
The books that tell lies
The book of discretion
Despite such desecration
They didn't write in their books
The books that demonise us
The ones that glorified our tormentors' ways
Go say it loudly
So demands the story of stories

Go tell how our names were crucified
Ay
They were crucified on the cross with our cultures
Aren't we their saviours?
They didn't put our felled names in their books
They treated us like a curse
We didn't know they were crooks!
We didn't know they were criminals
Sinners and liars
Now, we know detail
Why don't we rebel?

Poses the story of stories
Do we need the nerves of steel?
To rebel against this internalised self-destruction
It is but our obligation
It only needs our determination
To fight against this degradation
We are just like any other homo sapiens
Therefore, we can fight for our self-possession
Let's do it now
Just now
Time is now
We have nothing to lose
Come join hands
To tell our story of stories

Tell this story with liveliness
Tell it with self-assurance
This is your story
This is your duty
To tell the very story
That tells your history
Feel no guiltiness
Nobody else
Will accurately tell your story
This is your story of stories

Tell the story even to the birdies
Let them fly with it in the skies
Tell it to the creepy-crawlies
Let them tell all creatures

Let the creation gallantly pronounce
That victims are no longer in chains
Foreign names we must denounce
Let tree hear the story of stories
Let even the devils here the story of stories
Aye
Tell the story of stories

Why African carry foreign names?
Why do foreigners not carry African names?
What's wrong with our African names?
Our beautiful and cute names
Nkwazi will never be James
Nesaa will never be Agnes
Nyerere will never be Julius
Mkisi can't be Abbas
Mshindi and Mukundi can't be Abu Nuwas
Bantu can't be Banu Abs
This is ridiculous
Let us dissect and detoxify the issue of names
What is in the names?
Why do we carry ridiculous foreign names?
Can they carry ours?
When will they do that?
When will they reciprocate?
Why foreign names?
Quips the story of stories

They treated us like stones

We aren't rivers or mountains given names
Can they decline while they don't have brains?
How, if at all, they are notions?
We are humans endowed with big brains
Super humans of course
No doubt about this
This is what it is
We are blessed with super intuitions
Like any other humans
We are humans
Let's refuse to be objectified
Like the story of stories tells us
Factual story of stories

Let us tell it with pride
Yea, our story is our pride
That is the only qualification it needs
Never feel insignificant
When you tell this story
It is your story
It is even holy
Holier than gory stories
Stand up and tell your story
Let even birds hear your story
Show its significance
The story of stories

I am asking those who superimposed names on us
Ay, I would like to hear their explanations

I would like to ask them some questions
I have them in millions
Aye, the questions our people failed to ask
I'll never fail to ask
I'll ask again and again
I need the right answers
Why carrying foreign and ridiculous names?
Didn't we have names before?
Every victim must hark
Must hark the story of stories

This story is your treasure
Tell it with self-composure
Enjoy its aura
When it feels the atmosphere
Let every hear it
Let all know it
Never hide it
Never feel ashamed about it
It is your duty to tell it
It is your sacred duty to defend it
No one else will defend the story
The story of stories

Goofy and Spoofy Languages

When our tormentors came
They brought their colonial languages
They forcefully introduced their jargons
Through them they maligned us
They called us savages and all kinds of names
They forgot that they were the very true savages
They committed indescribable savagery
Didn't they introduce slavery?
Didn't they commit thuggery?
Didn't they used chicanery?
Wasn't that tomfoolery?
Everything they brought was in their languages
They spread it at expenses of our protolanguages
Did we twig their tongues?
Did we ponder on the damages?
Nope we didn't
We even have never bothered about it
Yet, we value them more than our own languages!
Despite knowing that
They did everything in their wicked languages
Did we know what they said?
How will you know?
Ask the story of stories

Our tormentors taught us to rave
We abused our languages
We recited their languages

We negated ours
Some still don't want to speak their languages
So marvels the story of stories

We were taught to pray in foreign languages
'God's books' were written in foreign languages
It is as if their god doesn't understand our languages
Yea
Indeed, their gods don't understand our languages
How can their gods understand our languages?
If their gods could not see our humanity
How could they know our languages?
They gods know everything except our languages
One thing their God knows is our moneys
Whenever we give them offerings
They don't complain the God doesn't appreciate our currencies
Quips the story of stories

Those who superimposed their languages on us
They degraded and demonised our languages
They also called us savages
When will we demystify these scrapings?
Who among us?
Through their languages
We were robbed
Through their languages
We were duped
Do we need to maintain the *status quo*?

That is *sine qua non*
It is close to a call
Tell the story of stories

We were taught Latin
Then, there came Arabic
Before then
There came brutish British with their ridiculous English
There followed ever deceptive French
Thereafter, there came brutal Spanish
Don't forget merciless Portuguese
Now, we are learning Chinese
Do they learn our languages?
Why should they
If they do is for spying us
Says the story of stories

Foreign languages cuckolded our people
They mistook them with knowledge
Our rulers like to speak foreign languages
To indicate they are educated
They glorify these languages
As they look down at theirs
Their language is the language of self-hate
So says the story of stories

Although I use it to communicate this truth
What else can I do?
Can't my Swahili not do?

How about Shona and Zulu?
I know they can do
Again, how if they are not universalised?
How if they are not accepted?
This is your challenge
My challenge
Our challenge
So admonishes the story of stories

Our Identity

When our tormentors came
They did a great harm
The first casualty was our identity
We lost it
They robbed us of our identity
They superimposed on us their sham identity
Instead of being Africans
We became Christians
We became Muslims
We became Baptists
We became Mennonites
They referred to us as animists
Animists!
Who brought animality?
Who committed bestiality?
We never committed paederasty
Never has it been a part of ancestry
We strictly stuck to morality
This is nothing but truth
Go excavate the story of stories

We were taught to deny our personality
Some ran away from their colour
They embark on skin whitening
In this they see no error
To them, fake beauty is an in-thing
They gobble every garbage blindly
They believe timorously

As if they are brainless
Quips the story of the stories

Colonisers duped our unsuspecting ancestors
Those they wrongly thought that were partners
became their tormentors
Those they wrongly thought that equal were
criminals
They became their colonisers
They destroyed our mores
This is what cultural imperialism did to them
Do they know the dangers they are courting?
Who will help them out of this suffering?
Is it an office-bearer?
They called themselves civilisers
Were they civilisers?
Ask the story of stories

For the first time
The cloned politicians
A politician failed a long time ago
Since independence, I see nothing
I only see do nothing politicians
Only they do is to enjoy bingo
Yeah, bingo after election rigging
They dupe the citizenry
Those who vote for them
What do they offer them?
Openly vending them!
Ask the story of stories

Racism

What different do tormentors have from any
gooey dingo?
Don't they smell badly like mungos mungo?
Remind yourselves of their pong
Dingoes are even innocent
We accuse them of greed
Remember they are beasts
How do we call greedy people?
Victims ran away from themselves
They willingly chose to be slaves
Ay, the slaves of their deceivers
It see this as a sort of violence
Aye, colonisation is violence
Alongside colonialism is racism

Racism is violence
Racism is cancerous
Even though it doesn't use any gyve
Upon us it behoove
To fight violence
It is a creature of ignorance
It is a very bad mental disease
Its magnitude is grave
Consider this
How humans discriminate against others?
What difference does it make from monsters?
Don't we share the same nature?

Ask the story of stories

What should we call prejudice?
Is it not the product of ignorance?
What is it?
If it is not a type of disease
What is it?
I would like to know it
Victims discriminate against their custom
Either out of ignorance or out of the venom of religion
Yet, foreign religions accepted is as a norm
Isn't this inculcating self-discrimination?
Isn't this self-degradation?
Ask the story of stories

What should we call it?
Please, name this dishonesty
We need to give it a right name
Is it not criminality?
Is it not barbarity?
what is its right name?
Ironically, the same don't discriminate against animals
I see white people with black animals
Black dogs
Black hogs
Do you like their pong?
They even eat black figs!
Don't they swig black Modelo Negra
Testifies the story of stories

The colour has never been a problem
The problem is s/he who's assigned blackness
This is against intellectual norm
It is nothing but ignorance
Yes, racism is psychosis
Racism is but bunkum
What a venom
I fear it like leprosy
I hate it lake curse
Please all sane people must fight racism
Fight any rotten ism
Stipulates the story of stories

Racism like colonialism is iniquity
Have I said it is barbarity?
It is more than that
Colonialism is debility
On the frail can harbour it
Colonial is criminality
Be it political or cultural
It is next to animality
Yes, under whatever rationale
Colonialism is but barbarity
It is evil for humanity
Says the story of stories

Self-denialism is nothing but self-deception
It is only a clown
The one who can spin

Whatever s/he puts hands on
Otherwise, self-denialism is a sin
I didn't know I would live to see
To see people denying their existence
Too, see people running away from themselves
Yes, I surely did not expect this irreverence
Here I am in a surprise
How grave it is
Ask the story of stories

It was hard to understand and believe
How some humans incongruously behave
Those who accused others of being creatures of cave
While they are cave people themselves
Especially, in the twenty first century
Did you expect to evidence it?
Think about that
Let us share whatever we get
How do you talk about it?
Here we are
Says the story of stories

I see people running from themselves
They even hate themselves
What does this have?
It has nothing but grieves
The state of denial is the only thing they face
They are afraid of their languages
They are afraid of their delicious foods
Yet, they devour and worship foreign junk foods!

Look at how they grow pots
Is it why we're taught to pray for them before eating them?
Did the farmers pray for them before they're produced?
Did they pray for our land?
Who cursed our foods?
Queries the story of stories

Bible Vs Land

If there's book we need to hold accountable
This is none other than the bible
However horrible
Yea
Horrible and gullible
Our tormentors came with a bible
Yes
The bible
They called it a holy bible
Was it holy or horrible?
The latter is the reply
When we met
They put the bible before us
They openly opened it to dupe us
Without they had nothing to hide from us
We wrongly thought they're transparent
Before long
They told us to close our eyes
Our land was gone
The bible was in our hands!

Using their horrible bible
They asserted
With it
Impossible is possible
They said the bible was the word of God
We didn't ask which God!
They gave us the bible
In exchange, they took our land

Yet, we've never understood
Why exchanging land with word
Can anybody cultivate anything in the word?
Marvels the story of stories

They say we pray for everything so to be blessed!
They badly seek salvation!
Where did they get contamination?
They gave us the bible and took our land
Our situation became horrible and hard
They became unimaginably moneyed
Then, they said that was right
They gave themselves the rights to take our rights
Then, they came back teaching us human rights!
Thereafter, hanged our Kings and Queens
They said it was good
Do they pray for their GMO foods?
These might need prayers
They need to be blessed
Their dangers are huge
They are cursed
This is the story of stories

They produce junk
Then, they export to us
Our seeds they have sank
They've always had us to zonk
They have never stopped to twank
When ours become zilch
We behave like an ostrich

We hide our heads in the sands
Says the story of stories

They taught us to sing their hail
Yes
We praise their so-called holy conurbations
We go there to pledge our adherence
We swear by their deities
We venerate their fake clerics and mystics
Some swear by these foreign conurbations
They believe and call them holy conurbations
Aren't our cities holy?
We spend billions on going there
Ask the story of stories

We sing praise for their greatness
We do so at the detriment of our losses
We believe in their story
They don't believe in ours
They taught us to believe
Yes
We believe without understanding
We were taught to accept everything
Never shall we question
This is what mental slavery means
Says the story of stories

We praise their foods
Don't our waters heal?
We ignore ours

We feed them with our foods
They feed us with their words
Some even believe in their waters
They call them healing waters
Some postulate towards their cities
When will they face ours?
Ask the story of stories

Some taught us even how to dress
They taught us how to clean ourselves
Did they find us dirty?
Didn't we know how to do that?
They treated us like animals
They think they brought everything
Yes,
Everything 'good'
All in the name of Deity
They turned us into hunts
Says the story of stories

They called our cultures diabolical
What of our food and land?
What about our minerals?
What about our natural riches?
Isn't this a double standard?
Our people gullibly swallowed all such garbage
They were taught to hate everything
Yes, everything meaningful
Then, they said it is pog!
It was like bogof

Yes, bogof in commerce
They believed everything they owned was sinful
Yet, they embraced self-destruction
This is the story of stories

Mental Slavery

We were given toxic education
Education full of chains
Education for self-annihilation
Education full of deprivation
They called their education formal
Ours became informal
Theirs became modern
Ours became traditional
Ours was but practical education
We learned and taught through doing
Theirs became purely colonial and fictional
Colonial education
Colonial religions
Here we are forsaken
Foreigners corrupted our people
They taught them to run away from themselves
They created fake people
Those who cannot think for themselves
Yet, they asserted they civilised our beloved people
Against the story of stories

They have always had us to spoof
Since we made a goof
Any of us is but a noof
Do you want any proof?
Yes, they think we are all doofs
Let's show them we are real buffs
Let's committedly and in unison say 'nuff is 'nuff

They've always played it rough
Even if it demands us to be tough
These are the only stuff
To hell with any of their belief
Says the story of stories

Let us cut their intellectual cuffs
We are not like calves
We are mature 'nuff
For the task, we're up to snuff
Even if it begs for a miff
Let's remove their niff
let us do it with a boff
We are tired of their duff
Avers the story of stories

Some of our people are afraid of themselves
What cowards and slaves!
They discriminate against themselves
Yet, they discriminate against those of theirs
They discriminate against themselves
Is it not folly?
When an adult behaves like a jolly
Jolly!
Are they under the effects of molly?
Gory!
Isn't this cultural bully?
Under their deception
They received everything willy-nilly
Ask the story of stories

I am not a polly
Neither am I a son of 'holy' molly
Why treating me like a tolly?
Am I mentally a tolly?
Stop this archaic folly
What should we call self-denialism?
Some think it is modernism
Is it not barbarism?
Golly!
Olly
Go tell the story of stories

Let us explore their behaviours
They are amidst us
They are everywhere
Yes, otherwise
They hate their traditions
They devour those of others
They hate their brethren
Then, they love foreigners
Charity begins home
Everybody has a place to call home
Your home is your home
Their home is their home
Says the story of stories

When charity fails at home
We call it a doom
That is not your home
Even if you call it home
This is a norm

Of those who spell doom
Those who hate their names
By taking foreign ones
those whom sometimes
We may deem
Insane
Says the story of stories

Those who abuse their own ways of life
Simply because they blindly and wrong believe
They uninformedly believe that they are evil
That is their evil gospel
Are their ways really evil?
Evil are their ignorance
Evil is their mental abeyance
Evil is their arrogance
Evil is their negligence
We need to forgive and educate them
Says the story of stories

Why don't they comprehend
The same gospel is the way of other people
The difference from there is it is promoted
Whereas there are demonized
In the end, they all socially constructed
Belief has become a mental graveyard
Sometimes, it is even awkward
Hard to comprehend
When a human becomes a clod
Through s/he is abused
Notes the stories of stories

In the Name of God

Everything our tormentors did
It was done in the name of God
What a racist god!
Our religions were felled
Our noble cultures were despised
They treated us like dogs
Their god did and said nothing
Should we endure abuses in the name of God?
Racism in the name of God
Everything in the name of God
Which God?
God of offends
Religion has become a clad
Or call it a cloud
In it, gory becomes holy
It makes me sometimes ogle!
What an ogre!
Says the story of stories

As unsuspecting followers
We've always ran to the bottom
As if we've no gist of wisdom
They fed us with all sorts of bunkum
Let's shun this bunkum
They spelt our intellectual doom
When they invented academic monopoly
They inculcated ignorance in us
In the name of education
What kind of education was it?

If it did not iterate us
So quips the story of stories

They denied us of freedom
Through their criminal schemes
They turned our Empires and Kingdoms into
fiefdoms
Our knowledges had no room
Our intellectuality became doomy
Every black person was made a booby
Now that we are able
Let us reclaim our wisdom
This is the right time
Religions have burdened and corrupted many
individuals
Our people are in a front pew
They swallow whatever religions spew
Do they know they are in mental gaols?
Please, read the story of stories

Many have been hypnotised
To be precise they're brainwashed
They act like androids
As if they have no brains
Their natural abilities of thinking have been
removed
They think using a collective borrowed and blurred
mind
They regurgitate whatever their masters to them
inculcated
That is done without critical mind

How do we help such doomed people?
They were taught to receive and eat the word
Who can survive on word?
Ironically, those feeding others with a word
Do not depend on the word!
We need to be against wayward
Admonishes the story of stories

Africa that used to feed everybody
Is, like a nobody, now fed
Is laughed at by everybody!
What a fad!
Shame on everybody!
What did we get from the word?
The word starved us
The word made them plush
To hell with the word
It brought dearth
They told us our salvation was through bloodshed
Yes, the blood of the brood of the Lord
Yes, the brood of the lamb of God
The one who 'died' for the world
Though he could not save himself
As per the story of stories

Why did they shed our blood?
Why did they exploit our toil?
Aren't we their saviours?
Why are we then deceived?
We are their true saviours
Our land saved them

Our minerals saved them
How poor would they be without colonising us?
How poor would they be without enslaving us?
How rich would we be without them robbing us?
Quips the story of stories

They say he saved us and the world
If so, why aren't victims saved?
Are poor fellas saved?
Is the world truly saved?
Is Africa saved?
Why did God forget during slavery?
Why his people enslaved Africans?
Why did they colonise Africans?
Are Africans practically saved
Are we practically saved?
If so, why do they still count sins on us?
Which sins did this guy take?
Who took his sins?
Who also created sins?
Ask the story of stories

Sinners called us sinners
Against whom did we sin?
Didn't they sin against us?
Why didn't we call them sinners?
This is their right tag
Yes, the enslaved us
They colonised us
They lied to us
The abused us

They even still do
Ask the story of stories

The sinners became saviours
And the innocents were made sinners
This has gone on
We don't even know as of now
If sinners assign the classification
Who then are true sinners?
Are we truly sinners?
If we are, then
Who are they?
These are just sinners who called others the sinners
Is it not an irony?
Ask the story of stories

So Long

I say so long to all
I thus say *kwaheri* to Central and East Africa
Hamba kahle for our Zulu brethren in South Africa
Sara mushe to our Brethren in Zimbabwe
Haa gongol our pals in Senegal
Sala hantle to our family in Lesotho
Nabadi gelyo our friends in Somalia
Ma' uk ged to our friends in Djibouti
Naagatti in Ethiopia
Gue ngozi to our friends in the CAR
Natiki bino to our friends in the DRC
Sala kakuhle to our Xhosa kinfolks
Tsamaya sentle to the good people of Botswana

Goodbye to our English speakers
Zài jiàn to our Chinese speakers
Au revoir to our French *évolues* wherever you are
Tiwonana our beloved friends in Malawi
Adios amigos to our amigos in Angola, Guinea-Bissau and Mozambique
Veloma to our good people of Madagascar
Ma'ssalaam to Arabic speaking Africans
Ban kwana to our Nigerian friends
Be bennen yon to our Yoruba friends
Foo watido to our great friends of the Gambia
All that I am unable to touch base with
Please forgive me
Nonetheless, take it from me
We are in this together
For, we've been suffering together
And we must be liberated together
Always together
Let us exhume and tell the story of stories together
It is our butchered noble story
Forever together

Mmap New African Poets Series

If you have enjoyed *The Stories of our Stories*, consider these other fine books in the **Mmap New African Poets** Series from *Mwanaka Media and Publishing*:

I Threw a Star in a Wine Glass by Fethi Sassi
Best New African Poets 2017 Anthology by Tendai R Mwanaka and Daniel Da Purificacao
Logbook Written by a Drifter by Tendai Rinos Mwanaka
Mad Bob Republic: Bloodlines, Bile and a Crying Child by Tendai Rinos Mwanaka
Zimbolicious Poetry Vol 1 by Tendai R Mwanaka and Edward Dzonze
Zimbolicious Poetry Vol 2 by Tendai R Mwanaka and Edward Dzonze
Zimbolicious: An Anthology of Zimbabwean Literature and Arts, Vol 3 by Tendai Mwanaka
Under The Steel Yoke by Jabulani Mzinyathi
Fly in a Beehive by Thato Tshukudu
Bounding for Light by Richard Mbuthia
Sentiments by Jackson Matimba
Best New African Poets 2018 Anthology by Tendai R Mwanaka and Nsah Mala
Words That Matter by Gerry Sikazwe
The Ungendered by Delia Watterson
Ghetto Symphony by Mandla Mavolwane
Sky for a Foreign Bird by Fethi Sassi
A Portrait of Defiance by Tendai Rinos Mwanaka
Zimbolicious: An Anthology of Zimbabwean Literature and Arts, Vol 4 by Tendai Mwanaka and Jabulani Mzinyathi

When Escape Becomes the only Lover by Tendai R Mwanaka
وَيَسْهَرُ اللَّيْلُ عَلَى شَفَتِي...وَالغَمَام by Fethi Sassi
A Letter to the President by Mbizo Chirasha
This is not a poem by Richard Inya
Pressed flowers by John Eppel
Righteous Indignation by Jabulani Mzinyathi:
Blooming Cactus by Mikateko Mbambo
Rhythm of Life by Olivia Ngozi Osouha
Travellers Gather Dust and Lust by Gabriel Awuah Mainoo
Chitungwiza Mushamukuru: An Anthology from Zimbabwe's Biggest Ghetto Town by Tendai Rinos Mwanaka
Zimbolicious: An Anthology of Zimbabwean Literature and Arts, Vol 5 by Tendai Mwanaka
Because Sadness is Beautiful? by Tanaka Chidora
Of Fresh Bloom and Smoke by Abigail George
Shades of Black by Edward Dzonze
Best New African Poets 2020 Anthology by Tendai Rinos Mwanaka, Lorna Telma Zita and Balddine Moussa
This Body is an Empty Vessel by Beaton Galafa
Between Places by Tendai Rinos Mwanaka
Best New African Poets 2021 Anthology by Tendai Rinos Mwanaka, Lorna Telma Zita and Balddine Moussa
Zimbolicious: An Anthology of Zimbabwean Literature and Arts, Vol 6 by Tendai Mwanaka and Chenjerai Mhondera
A Matter of Inclusion by Chad Norman
Keeping the Sun Secret by Mariel Awendit
سِجِلٌّ مَكْتُوبٌ لِثَائِه by Tendai Rinos Mwanaka
Ghetto Blues by Tendai Rinos Mwanaka
Zimbolicious: An Anthology of Zimbabwean Literature and Arts, Vol 7 by Tendai Rinos Mwanaka and Tanaka Chidora

Best New African Poets 2022 Anthology by Tendai Rinos Mwanaka and Helder Simbad
Dark Lines of History by Sithembele Isaac Xhegwana
a sky is falling by Nica Cornell
Death of a Statue by Samuel Chuma
Along the way by Jabulani Mzinyathi
Strides of Hope by Tawanda Chigavazira
Young Galaxies by Abigail George
Coming of Age by Gift Sakirai
Mother's Kitchen and Other Places by Antreka. M. Tladi
Best New African Poets 2023 Anthology by Tendai Rinos Mwanaka, Helder Simbad and Gerald Mpesse
Zimbolicious Anthology Vol 8 by Tendai Rinos Mwanaka and Mathew T Chikono
Broken Maps by Riak Marial Riak
Formless by Raïs Neza Boneza
Of poets, gods, ghosts. Irritants and storytellers by Tendai Rinos Mwanaka
Ethiopian Aliens by Clersidia Nzorozwa
In The Inferno by Jabulani Mzinyathi
Who Told You To Be God by Mariel Awendit
Nobody Loves Me by Abigail George

www.ingramcontent.com/pod-product-compliance
Lightning Source LLC
Chambersburg PA
CBHW070939180426
43192CB00039B/2356